Homeland Secuirty: Fiscal Years 2014-2018 Strategic Plan

This page intentionally left blank

MESSAGE FROM THE SECRETARY

I am pleased to submit the U.S. Department of Homeland Security (DHS) Strategic Plan for Fiscal Years (FY) 2014-2018, fulfilling the GPRA Modernization Act of 2010 (P. L. 111-352) and the Office of Management and Budget's (OMB) Circular A-11, Part 6 (2013) requirement for all Federal departments and agencies to publish an Agency Strategic Plan.

Much like the 2014 Quadrennial Homeland Security Review, the FY14-18 Strategic Plan provides an analytic foundation for the Department's Unity of Effort Initiative. The DHS Unity of Effort Initiative builds important linkages between the Department's planning, programming, budgeting, and execution processes, ensuring that the Department invests and operates in a cohesive, unified fashion, and makes decisions that are transparent and collaborative to drive strategic guidance to results. The FY14-18 Strategic Plan represents an important step in our process toward achieving unity of effort by articulating the strategies we employ to achieve each goal and long-term performance measures that we use to evaluate our progress.

As part of the development of this Strategic Plan, the Department also undertook an unprecedented effort to identify the Department's highest priorities across mission areas. While we will continue to execute against all of the mission goals and objectives laid out in the 2014 Quadrennial Homeland Security Review and the 2014-2018 Strategic Plan, these areas represent our top priorities in terms of investment, strategic and operational planning, and stakeholder engagement. By prioritizing efforts in this way, we will be more closely aligned in our efforts, stronger partners to our stakeholders, and better stewards of our limited resources.

While the 2014 QHSR focused on our shared responsibilities with partners across the federal, state, local, tribal, and territorial governments, the private sector, and other nongovernmental organizations, the FY14-18 Strategic Plan focuses on how we accomplish our mission as a Department. This report reflects the important work of all homeland security employees, who tirelessly fulfill the missions of homeland security: prevent terrorism and enhance security, secure and manage our borders, enforce and administer our immigration laws, safeguard and secure cyberspace, and strengthen national preparedness and resilience. I am continually grateful for their service.

Sincerely,

Jeh Charles Johnson

This page intentionally left blank

Credit: U.S. Department of Homeland Security

OVERVIEW

The United States is poised at the outset of a new era in homeland security that reflects long-term changes in the security environment and key advances in homeland security capabilities. The 2014 Quadrennial Homeland Security Review describes the challenges and opportunities of this new era and how the Department of Homeland Security (DHS) and our homeland security partners must strategically posture ourselves to address those challenges. The 2014 Quadrennial Homeland Security Review also takes an important foundational step toward a Secretary-level priority: strengthening Departmental "Unity of Effort." The DHS Unity of Effort Initiative builds important linkages between the Department's planning, programming, budgeting, and execution processes, ensuring that the Department invests and operates in a cohesive, unified fashion, and makes decisions that are transparent and collaborative to drive the Secretary's strategic guidance to results.

The DHS FY14-18 Strategic Plan focuses on how we will implement the goals laid out in the 2014 Quadrennial Homeland Security Review. It describes the missions and goals of homeland security, the strategies we use to achieve those goals, and the ways in which we measure our success. It also sets several key, priority efforts under each mission and describes how those priorities will be achieved through the DHS Unity of Effort Initiative.

The Homeland Security vision is a homeland that is safe, secure, and resilient against terrorism and other hazards, where American interests, aspirations, and way of life can thrive. This requires the dedication of more than 240,000 employees in jobs that range from aviation and border security to emergency response, from cybersecurity analysis to chemical facility inspections. Our duties are wide-ranging, but our goal is clear — keeping America safe. The 2014 Quadrennial Homeland Security Review reaffirmed the five-mission structure of DHS:

- Prevent Terrorism and Enhance Security

- Secure and Manage our Borders

- Enforce and Administer Our Immigration Laws

- Safeguard and Secure Cyberspace; and

- Strengthen National Preparedness and Resilience

Accomplishing these missions requires unity of effort – across every area of DHS activity and among the numerous homeland security partners and stakeholders.

UNITY OF EFFORT

The Department has many strengths, including the professionalism, skill, and dedication of its people and the rich history and tradition of its Components, which have led to many successes over the Department's relatively short life. The Unity of Effort Initiative capitalizes on these strengths while identifying ways to enhance the cohesion of the Department as a whole. The Department will accomplish this not by centralizing the decision making authority and processes within an opaque DHS Headquarters, but rather by transparently incorporating DHS Components into unified decision making processes and the analytic efforts that inform decision making.

We will focus initially on four main lines of effort to improve our planning, programming, budgeting and execution processes: 1) inclusive senior leader discussion and decision making forums that provide an environment of trust and transparency; 2) strengthened management processes for investment, including requirements, budget, and acquisition processes that look at cross-cutting issues across the Department; 3) focused,

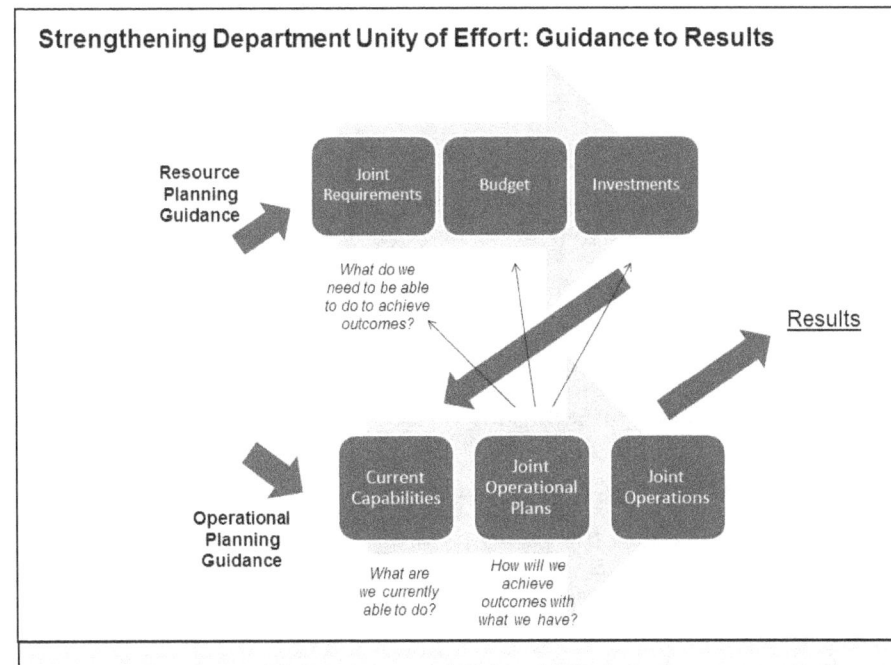

Strengthening Department Unity of Effort: Guidance to Results

Resource Planning Guidance

Joint Requirements

Budget

Investments

What do we need to be able to do to achieve outcomes?

Results

Operational Planning Guidance

Current Capabilities

Joint Operational Plans

Joint Operations

What are we currently able to do?

How will we achieve outcomes with what we have?

Figure 1: Strengthening Departmental Unity of Effort diagram

collaborative Departmental strategy, planning, and analytic capability that support more effective DHS-wide decision making and operations; and 4) enhanced coordinated operations to harness the significant resources of the Department more effectively.

If executed properly, the Unity of Effort Initiative will provide the Department with better understanding of the broad and complex DHS mission space and support the effective execution of our missions.

STAKEHOLDER ENGAGEMENT

The FY14–18 DHS Strategic Plan builds upon the stakeholder engagement and outreach process conducted for the 2014 Quadrennial Homeland Security Review and incorporates the more specific consultation requirements set forth in the GPRA Modernization Act of 2010. Throughout the Quadrennial Homeland Security Review process, DHS conducted extensive engagement with federal executive branch partners and Congress; state, local, tribal and territorial partners; the private sector; academics, and others. In addition to those engagements, development of the FY14-18 Strategic Plan has been closely coordinated with the Office of Management and Budget.

CROSS-AGENCY PRIORITY GOALS

Cross-Agency Priority goals address the longstanding challenge of tackling horizontal problems across vertical organizational silos. To establish these goals, the Office of Management and Budget solicited nominations from Federal agencies and several congressional committees. Per the GPRA Modernization Act of 2010 requirement to address Cross-Agency Priority Goals in the agency strategic plan, the annual performance plan, and the annual performance report, please refer to http://www.performance.gov for the Department of Homeland Security's contributions to those goals and progress, where applicable. The Department currently contributes to the following mission-related Cross-Agency Priority Goals:

- Cybersecurity (related to DHS Objective 4.2: Secure the Federal Civilian Government Information Technology Enterprise).

- Climate Change (Federal Actions) (related to DHS Objective 5.1: Enhance National Preparedness; DHS Objective 5.2: Mitigate Hazards and Vulnerabilities; and DHS Objective 5.3: Ensure Effective Emergency Response).

- Insider Threat and Security Clearance (related to DHS Objective 1.1: Prevent Terrorist Attacks; DHS Objective 1.3: Reduce Risk to the Nation's Critical Infrastructure, Key Leadership, and Events; and Maturing and Strengthening Homeland Security).

- Job-Creating Investment (related to Maturing and Strengthening Homeland Security).

- Infrastructure Permitting Modernization (related to Maturing and Strengthening Homeland Security).

- Science, Technology, Engineering and Mathematics Education (related to Maturing and Strengthening Homeland Security).

The DHS FY14-18 Strategic Plan is a Departmental management tool for strategic achievement of the responsibilities set forth in those documents. The Plan satisfies the requirements of the GPRA Modernization Act of 2010 (P. L. 111-352) and the Office of Management and Budget's Circular A-11 requirement to publish an Agency Strategic Plan.

CONTACT INFORMATION

Department strategic capstone products are located at our public website at http://www.dhs.gov/qhsr. For more information, contact

Department of Homeland Security
Office of Policy
Office of Strategy, Planning, Analysis, and Risk
Washington, D.C. 20528

Information may also be requested by sending an email to STRATEGY@dhs.gov.

TABLE OF CONTENTS

This page intentionally left blank

ANALYTIC AGENDA

The Department of Homeland Security, like any large government agency or private corporation, must be able to harness vast amounts of data to inform strategy and future planning. As the latter sections of this plan describe, there are a number of key areas where DHS must improve its ability to collect new data, analyze existing data, and present data in a compelling way to our partners and the public. The Department's four-year Analytic Agenda provides the foundation for tackling this "Big Data" challenge and supporting analytically-informed decision-making across DHS missions.

Over the past several years, the Department has made great strides to improve its analytical understanding of the diverse DHS mission space. For example, DHS developed and fostered a risk community of interest, convening risk management experts from across the Department to share risk data and best practices for risk assessment. To further support the Secretary's Unity of Effort Initiative, the Department will deepen its analytic capability across its mission areas. In particular, DHS will continue to acquire, develop, and implement the basic tools required for data-driven management of its missions, such as the ability to consistently assess strategic/external risk; measure outcomes; forecast such outcomes under different resource allocations, policies, and economic conditions; and use these forecasts to inform strategic planning, programming, acquisition, and operational decisions.

To begin building this capability, DHS Headquarters will, in close coordination with departmental and enterprise partners, formalize a line of effort similar in purpose to the Department of Defense's "Analytic Agenda" initiative. The objective of this multi-year effort will be to build and institutionalize the necessary data, models, and underlying business processes to provide a unified baseline for aiding decision-making across the Department. Topics for these analytic baselines will be determined by leadership, based on missions or goals that would benefit from a more rigorous analytical approach. Key inputs informing the topic selection are the Quadrennial Homeland Security Review, this DHS Strategic Plan, ongoing analysis of changes in the strategic environment, annual resource and operational planning guidance, and other DHS policy imperatives.

For any particular mission area, an analytic agenda may include comprehensive empirical modeling; estimation of the impacts of social, technological, economic, environmental, or political variables; incorporation of these empirical results into a model with the capability to simulate future outcomes; sustained development of outcome measurement; and development of dashboards and tools for support to strategic-level decision-making. Such an effort would enable the creation of a full set of performance measures for a given study topic; support analytically informed strategy development, resource allocation, investment, and operational decision making for that topic; facilitate systematic program evaluation; and optimally deliver indicator and warning capabilities to allow the Department to assume an anticipatory posture. Maintaining a standing set of empirical models would allow the Department to quickly analyze the causes, likely duration, and the predicted effectiveness of alternative policy options in response to new trends. DHS would use this data to develop effective strategies and communicate authoritatively with its public and private stakeholders.

The Analytic Agenda initiative will be co-led by the Office of Policy and the Office of the Chief Financial Officer, with each study leveraging the expertise of DHS Components. These offices will be responsible for setting the strategic direction, creating planning scenarios, identifying methodologies, conducting individual studies, providing data, warehousing that data and accompanying analytic results, and integrating the effort with the various DHS decision systems.

Credit: U.S. Coast Guard

DEPARTMENT MISSIONS AND GOALS

The first QHSR report developed an enduring mission framework for homeland security; that framework was reflected in the Fiscal Years 2012–2016 DHS Strategic Plan. As a preparatory activity for the second Quadrennial Homeland Security Review, the Department initiated an internal Roles and Missions Review to review and validate the Quadrennial Homeland Security Review 2010 mission framework. The Department updated the framework to reflect changes in policy, strategy, and the strategic environment. Activities previously categorized as "Providing Essential Support to National and Economic Security" were incorporated into the five homeland security missions and into the cross-cutting summary of activities documented in the Mature and Strengthen the Department section of the Strategic Plan. While the Quadrennial Homeland Security Review reflects an overarching strategic approach for homeland security, the DHS Strategic Plan reflects the strategies, including activities, programs, and operations, of the Department for executing our missions in the FY 2014–2018 timeframe.

Credit:: Transportation Security Administration

MISSION 1: PREVENT TERRORISM AND ENHANCE SECURITY

Preventing terrorism is the cornerstone of homeland security. Within this mission we focus on the goals of preventing terrorist attacks; preventing and protecting against the unauthorized acquisition or use of chemical, biological, radiological, and nuclear materials and capabilities; and reducing risk to the Nation's most critical infrastructure, key leaders, and events.

The 2014 Quadrennial Homeland Security Review described a more integrated, networked approach to counterterrorism and community engagement efforts. To improve overall Departmental unity of effort, we will work with our partners to identify, investigate, and interdict threats as early as possible; expand risk-based security; focus on countering violent extremism and preventing complex mass casualty attacks; reduce vulnerabilities by denying resources and targets; and uncover patterns and faint signals through enhanced data integration and analysis. DHS shares the responsibility to prevent terrorist attacks with several federal departments and agencies, including the Departments of State, Justice, and Defense, and the Office of the Director of National Intelligence, as well as with state, local, tribal, territorial, and private sector partners. DHS further collaborates with foreign partners on security issues of concern.

GOAL 1.1: PREVENT TERRORIST ATTACKS

The Department remains vigilant to new and evolving threats in order to protect the Nation from a terrorist attack. Although the U.S. Government's counterterrorism efforts have degraded the ability of al-Qa'ida's senior leadership in Afghanistan and Pakistan to centrally plan and execute sophisticated external attacks, since 2009 we have seen the rise of al-Qa'ida affiliates, such as al-Qa'ida in the Arabian Peninsula and the al-Nusrah Front in Syria. These groups have made attempts to export terrorism to our Nation. Additionally, we face the threat of domestic-based "lone offenders" and those who are inspired by violent extremist ideologies to radicalize and commit acts of terrorism against Americans and the Nation. These threats come in multiple forms and, because of the nature of independent actors, may be hardest to detect.

We will pursue the following strategies to prevent terrorist attacks:

Analyze, fuse, and disseminate terrorism information by sharing information with, and utilizing threat analysis alongside, stakeholders across the homeland security enterprise.

We remain committed to integrating critical data sources, such as those for biometric data, by consolidating or federating screening and vetting operations. We will also continually increase and integrate domain awareness capabilities, as well as improve our ability to fully utilize vast amounts of intelligence and other information—the so-called "big data" challenge—while rigorously protecting privacy and civil rights and civil liberties.

Deter and disrupt operations by leveraging the intelligence, information sharing, technological, operational, and policy-making elements within DHS to facilitate a cohesive and coordinated operational response. We will also develop intelligence sources and leverage research and analysis to identify and illustrate the tactics, behaviors, and indicators potentially associated with violent extremism as well as factors that may influence violent extremism, and jointly develop with federal, state, local, tribal, and territorial partners training for frontline law enforcement officers on behaviors that may be telling regarding violent extremist activity.

Strengthen transportation security by using a multi-layered risk-based approach to detect malicious actors and dangerous items at various entry and exit points in the travel and trade system. We will also improve coordination with foreign governments and stakeholders to expand pre-departure screening and enhance transportation security operations among willing partners to mitigate risks from overseas.

Counter violent extremism by: 1) supporting community-based problem solving and integration efforts, as well as local law enforcement programs; and 2) working with our partners to share information with frontline law enforcement partners, communities, families, and the private sector about how violent extremists are using the Internet and how to protect themselves and their communities.

GOAL 1.2: PREVENT AND PROTECT AGAINST THE UNAUTHORIZED ACQUISITION OR USE OF CHEMICAL, BIOLOGICAL, RADIOLOGICAL, AND NUCLEAR MATERIALS AND CAPABILITIES

Chemical, biological, radiological, and nuclear threats are enduring areas of concern. The consequences of these attacks are potentially high even though the likelihood of their occurrence is relatively low. Small scale chemical attacks are expected to remain more likely because the relative lack of specialized skills and knowledge required to conduct such attacks. However, nuclear terrorism and bioterrorism pose the most strategically significant risk because of their potential consequences. Although the difficulty of stealing a nuclear weapon or fabricating one from stolen or diverted weapons materials reduces the likelihood of this type of attack, the extremely high consequences of an improvised nuclear device attack make it an ongoing top homeland security risk.

We will pursue the following strategies to prevent and protect against the unauthorized acquisition or use of chemical biological, radiological, and nuclear materials and capabilities:

Anticipate chemical, biological, radiological, and nuclear emerging threats by identifying and understanding potentially dangerous actors, technologies, and materials, and prioritizing research and development activities including: 1) analyses of alternative technology options; 2) assessments of complex issues such as the relative risk of different chemical, biological, radiological, and nuclear threats; 3) experimentation and operational test and evaluation of technologies proposed for acquisition; 4) detailed technical characterization of potential biological threat organisms; 5) the creation of consensus standards that enable cost-effective progress across many fields; and 6) the determination of nuclear material characteristics through nuclear forensics techniques.

Identify and interdict unlawful acquisition and movement of chemical, biological, radiological, and nuclear precursors and materials by leveraging investigative and enforcement assets towards domestic and international movement of these materials and by engaging in information sharing with all stakeholders to monitor and control this technology.

Detect, locate, and prevent the hostile use of chemical, biological, radiological, and nuclear materials and weapons by 1) combining authorities and assets with other departments and agencies; 2) building the U.S. Government's global nuclear detection capability through the Global Nuclear Detection Architecture, a framework for detecting (through technical and non-technical means), analyzing, and reporting on nuclear and other radioactive materials that are out of regulatory control; 3) advancing nuclear forensics capabilities in order to close down nuclear smuggling networks, promote global nuclear security, and deter would-be nation state terrorist facilitators from transferring nuclear materials to terrorists; 4) providing unimpeachable forensic data for use by law enforcement authorities in the investigation and prosecution of crimes involving biological agents; 5) regulating high-risk chemical facilities to ensure that they take proper steps to mitigate risks; and 6) preventing the occurrence of significant biological incidents, where possible, but, when unable to prevent, stopping them from overwhelming the capacity of our state, local, tribal, and territorial partners to manage and respond. To this last point, DHS will deploy technologies that enable early detection of biological agents prior to the onset of symptoms, pursue more rapid responder capabilities, and increase the capacity and effectiveness of local public health, medical, and emergency services.

GOAL 1.3: REDUCE RISK TO THE NATION'S CRITICAL INFRASTRUCTURE, KEY LEADERSHIP, AND EVENTS

DHS has national leadership responsibility for enhancing security to the Nation's critical infrastructure and protecting key leaders, facilities, and National Special Security Events. DHS reduces risk across a wide portfolio of activities, including the agriculture and food sector, the travel and trade system, and the financial services sector. These systems are vulnerable to criminal exploitation and both physical and cyber-attacks. DHS also maintains constant guard over key leaders and during high-profile events, reducing the possibility that these events could be exploited by criminal or terrorist actors.

We will pursue the following strategies to reduce risk to the nation's critical infrastructure, key leadership, and events

Enhance security for the Nation's critical infrastructure from terrorism and criminal activity

Credit: U.S. Secret Service

by 1) identifying critical infrastructure and related vulnerabilities; 2) developing and deploying a scalable assessment methodology depending on the level of threat and the nature of the target; 3) inserting and/or developing appropriate technologies; 4) tracking protective measures of our partners across the homeland security enterprise; and 5) conducting investigations that maximize disruption of criminal enterprises that pose the greatest risk to the United States. We will also enhance the Nation's ability to counter improvise explosive devices (IEDs) by coordinating whole community efforts to prevent, protect against, respond to, and mitigate terrorist and criminal use of explosives.

Protect key leaders, facilities, and National Special Security Events by 1) working with partners across the homeland security enterprise to coordinate intelligence, information sharing, security, and response resources; 2) protecting the President, the Vice President, visiting heads of state, major Presidential candidates, and other designated protectees; 3) protecting federal facilities, employees, and visitors; and 4) assessing risk and coordinating support to partners during major special events across the Nation through the Special Events Assessment Rating.

HIGHLIGHTED PERFORMANCE MEASURES

The table below presents a subset of the DHS performance measures associated with gauging results for Mission 1. For more information on these measures, along with a more extensive list of measures associated with this mission, please see the FY 2013–2015 Annual Performance Report at http://www.dhs.gov/xabout/budget/editorial_0430.shtm.

Mission 1: Prevent Terrorism and Enhance Security				
Highlighted Performance Measures	Goal Alignment	Planned Targets		
		FY 2014	FY 2015	FY 2018
Percent of intelligence reports rated "satisfactory" or higher in customer feedback that enable customers to understand the threat (AO)	1.1	93%	94%	94%
Percent of foreign airports that serve as last points of departure and air carriers involved in international operations to the United States advised of necessary actions to mitigate identified vulnerabilities in order to ensure compliance with critical security measures (TSA)	1.1	100%	100%	100%
Percent of international air enplanements vetted against the terrorist watch list through Secure Flight (TSA)	1.1	100%	100%	100%
Percent of inbound air cargo screened on international passenger flights originating from outside the United States and Territories (TSA)	1.1	100%	100%	100%
Percent of cargo conveyances that pass through radiation portal monitors upon entering the nation via land border and international rail ports of entry (DNDO)	1.2	FOUO	FOUO	FOUO
Percent of performance standards implemented by the highest risk chemical facilities and verified by DHS (NPPD)	1.2	97%	95%	95%
Percent of total U.S. Secret Service protection activities that are incident-free for protection of national leaders, foreign dignitaries, designated protectees and others during travel or at protected facilities (USSS)	1.3	100%	100%	100%
Financial crimes loss prevented through a criminal investigation (in billions) (USSS)	1.3	$1.90	$2.70	$3.0

MISSION 2: SECURE AND MANAGE OUR BORDERS

Secure, well-managed borders must not only protect the United States against threats from abroad, they must also safeguard and expedite the flow of lawful trade and travel. Achieving this end requires that we focus on three interrelated goals: 1) secure U.S. air, land, and sea borders and approaches; 2) safeguard and expedite lawful trade and travel; and 3) disrupt and dismantle transnational criminal organizations and other illicit actors.

The 2014 Quadrennial Homeland Security Review defined a risk segmentation approach to managing the flows of people and goods: minimize disruption to and facilitate safe and secure inbound and outbound legal flows of people and goods; prioritize efforts to counter illicit finance and further increase transnational criminal organization perception of risk through targeted interdiction and other activities, while continuing to increase efficiencies in operations; and counter terrorist travel into the United States, terrorism against international travel and trade systems, and the export of sensitive goods and technology.

Building on that work, the U.S. Southern Border and Approaches Campaign Planning Effort (2014), one of the first management imperatives from the Unity of Effort Initiative, articulates four mutually-supporting key areas of effort for securing the southern border and approaches: 1) segment and expedite flows of people and goods at ports of entry; 2) strengthen the security and resilience of the global supply chain and the international travel system; 3) combat transnational organized crime and terrorism; and 4) prevent illegal flows of people and goods between ports of entry.

MISSION PRIORITIES

The following Mission Priorities represent the highest priority efforts for the Department of Homeland Security within Mission 2. While the Department will continue to work on all of the mission goals and objectives laid out in the 2014 Quadrennial Homeland Security Review and the 2014-2018 Strategic Plan, these are the top areas of focus in terms of investment, strategic and operational planning, and stakeholder engagement, and will be addressed through actions undertaken in one or more of the following DHS foundational activities: Joint Requirements Council, joint operational plans and operations, enhanced budget and investment processes, and focused strategic and analytic efforts.

- **Secure the U.S. Southern Border and approaches** by implementing a strategic framework.

- **Combat transnational organized crime** by countering illicit finance and further integrating elements of the layered defense.

GOAL 2.1: SECURE U.S. AIR, LAND, AND SEA BORDER AND APPROACHES

Flows of people and goods around the world have expanded dramatically in recent years. DHS employs a range of strategies to improve upon border security, as well as to exclude terrorist threats, drug traffickers, and other threats to national security, economic security, and public safety. DHS and our partners ensure transit via legal pathways; identify and remove people and goods attempting to travel illegally; and ensure the safety and integrity of these flows of people and goods by safeguarding the conveyances, nodes, and pathways that make up the travel and trade system. DHS relies on a combination of people, technology, assets (e.g., surface and aviation platforms), and infrastructure (e.g., roads, fences) across DHS operating components to enable situational awareness and secure the border. Given the inherently transnational nature of securing our borders, DHS also continues to build international partnerships to enhance our ability to identify threats or hazards before they emerge in the United States.

We will pursue the following strategies to secure U.S. air, land, and sea border and approaches:

Prevent illegal import and entry by employing a layered, risk-based approach to screen, identify, and intercept threats at points of departure and at U.S. ports of entry. Using a variety of intelligence, automated tools, and information collected in advance of arrival for passengers and cargo at air, land, and seaports, DHS screens, identifies, and intercepts threats at points of departure before they reach our borders. In the approaches to the United States, DHS maintains domain awareness efforts to establish and maintain a common operating picture of people, vehicles, aircraft, and marine vessels approaching our borders, as well as interdiction capabilities to achieve a law enforcement resolution.

Prevent illegal export and exit through a risk-based strategy to inspect people, cargo, and conveyances departing the United States through all airports, seaports, land border crossings, and international mail/courier facilities. Using this information, law enforcement organizations such as Immigration and Customs Enforcement will investigate illegal exports and exit.

GOAL 2.2: SAFEGUARD AND EXPEDITE LAWFUL TRADE AND TRAVEL

The vast majority of people and goods entering and exiting the United States represent lawful trade and travel. Lawful trade and travel provides enormous economic benefits to our society, evident by a substantial increase in the number of tourist and business travelers and in the value of U.S. exports and imports between 2005 and 2012, and underscored by projections for continued growth at an average of six percent annually through 2030. DHS and our partners work to secure and expedite these flows of people and goods, as they are a main driver of U.S. economic prosperity.

We will pursue the following strategies to safeguard and expedite lawful trade and travel:

Safeguard key nodes, conveyances, and pathways by establishing and enforcing security standards and plans that maintain or restore infrastructure capabilities to be resilient from attacks and natural disasters; this includes facilities at ports of entry, modes of transportation, and pathways.

Manage the risk of people and goods in transit by employing a risk-segmentation approach that identifies low-risk and high-risk people and goods moving within legal channels as far from the homeland as possible, and then expediting low-risk, lawful movement to and through the United States.

Maximize compliance with U.S. trade laws and promote U.S. economic security and competitiveness by: 1) working with international partners, such as the International Maritime Organization, the International Civil Aviation Organization, and INTERPOL, to create global standards for security and resilience of the global trade and travel system and 2) conducting cargo recognition programs to reduce redundancies for industry while maintaining a commensurate level of security.

GOAL 2.3: DISRUPT AND DISMANTLE TRANSNATIONAL CRIMINAL ORGANIZATIONS AND OTHER ILLICIT ACTORS

Transnational criminal organizations are increasing in strength and capability. They rely on revenues generated through the sale of illegal drugs and counterfeit goods, human trafficking and smuggling, and other criminal activities. They are also gaining strength by taking advantage of the same innovations in management and supply chain structures that are propelling multinational corporations.

We will pursue the following strategies to disrupt and dismantle transnational criminal organizations and other illicit actors:

Identify, investigate, disrupt, and dismantle TCOs by: 1) targeting illicit financing activities that transnational criminal organizations depend on, such as money laundering, and increasing outbound inspection to deter practices such as cash smuggling; and 2) creating a deterrent effect from injecting the greatest amount of uncertainty and concern into criminal decision making by swiftly shifting assets, presence, technology, and tools, further targeting and focusing interdiction activities, and emphasizing strategic communications that project the effectiveness of homeland security capabilities.

Disrupt illicit actors, activities, and pathways by using intelligence to target and interdict illicit people and goods through a rapid response workforce as well as surveillance and enforcement assets to detect, identify, monitor, track, and interdict targets of interest, and board vessels.

HIGHLIGHTED PERFORMANCE MEASURES

The table below presents a subset of the DHS performance measures associated with gauging results for Mission 2. For more information on these measures, along with a more extensive list of measures associated with this mission, please see the FY 2013–2015 Annual Performance Report at http://www.dhs.gov/xabout/budget/editorial_0430.shtm.

Mission 2: Secure and Manage Our Borders				
Highlighted Performance Measures	Goal Alignment	Planned Targets		
		FY 2014	FY 2015	FY 2018
Rate of interdiction effectiveness along the Southwest Border between ports of entry (CBP)	2.1	77%	80%	89%
Percent of people apprehended multiple times along the Southwest border (CBP)	2.1	≤ 17%	≤ 17%	≤ 17%
Number of smuggled outbound weapons seized at the ports of entry (CBP)	2.1	400	400	400
Percent of detected conventional aircraft incursions resolved along all borders of the United States (CBP)	2.1	100%	100%	100%
Percent of inbound cargo identified by CBP as potentially high-risk that is assessed or scanned prior to departure or at arrival at a U.S. port of entry (CBP)	2.2	100%	100%	100%
Percent of imports compliant with U.S. trade laws (CBP)	2.2	97.5%	97.5%	97.5%
Percent of import revenue successfully collected (CBP)	2.2	100%	100%	100%
Fishing regulation compliance rate (USCG)	2.2	96.5%	96.5%	97.5%
Number of detected incursions of foreign fishing vessels violating U.S. waters (USCG)	2.2	< 148	< 155	< 176
Percent of transnational gang investigations resulting in the disruption or dismantlement of high-threat transnational criminal gangs (ICE)	2.3	62%	62%	62%
Percent of transnational child exploitation or sex trafficking investigations resulting in the disruption or dismantlement of high-threat child exploitation or sex trafficking organizations or individuals (ICE)	2.3	25%	25%	25%

MISSION 3: ENFORCE AND ADMINISTER OUR IMMIGRATION LAWS

Immigration is essential to our identity as a nation of immigrants. Most American families have an immigration story, some recent, some more distant. Many immigrants have taken on great risks to work and contribute to America's prosperity or were provided refuge after facing persecution abroad. Americans are extremely proud of this tradition. Smart and effective enforcement and administration of our immigration laws remains a core homeland security mission.

The following priorities from the 2014 Quadrennial Homeland Security Review inform the strategic approach in this mission area: 1) Building a stronger, smarter border enforcement system; 2) Achieving smart and effective interior enforcement; 3) Creating a 21st-Century legal immigration system; 4) Facilitating reunions for long-separated families; 5) Creating an earned path to citizenship; and 6) Enhancing management and organization to develop a responsive immigration system.

GOAL 3.1: STRENGTHEN AND EFFECTIVELY ADMINISTER THE IMMIGRATION SYSTEM

At the center of any good immigration system must be a structure able to rapidly respond to regulatory changes and the flow of demand around the world while at the same time safeguarding security. We are constantly seeking ways to better administer benefits and use technology to make information more accessible and secure.

We will pursue the following strategies to strengthen and effectively administer the immigration system:

Promote lawful immigration by uniting families, providing refuge, fostering economic opportunity, and promoting citizenship. We will also work to better assist high-skilled immigrants, streamline the processing of immigrant visas to encourage businesses to grow in the United States, and develop innovative programs to enable immigrants to reach their potential in the United States.

Effectively administer the immigration services system by: 1) providing effective customer-oriented immigration benefit and information services at home and abroad; 2) making all information needed to make immigration decisions available to appropriate agencies electronically and in real-time, including active individual case files and biometric information; and 3) ensuring that only eligible applicants receive immigration benefits through expanded use of biometrics, a strengthening of screening processes, improvements to fraud detection, increases in legal staffing to ensure due process, and enhancements of interagency information sharing.

Promote the integration of lawful immigrants in American society by enhancing educational resources and promoting opportunities to increase understanding of U.S. civic principles and the rights, responsibilities, and importance of citizenship, and supporting comprehensive immigration reform that provides an earned pathway to citizenship.

GOAL 3.2: PREVENT UNLAWFUL IMMIGRATION

The increased movement of people and goods across our borders provides many opportunities but also provides more places for illegal goods, unauthorized migrants, and threats to hide. Unauthorized migration is influenced by many factors, including weak rule of law and violence in sending countries. In addition, violent extremists and criminals can hide within this larger flow of migrants who intend no harm.

We will pursue the following strategies to prevent unlawful immigration:

Prevent unlawful entry, strengthen enforcement, and reduce drivers of unlawful immigration by: 1) increasing situational awareness of our borders; 2) ensuring that only those abroad who are eligible receive travel documents to the United States; and 3) identifying and removing criminal aliens, individuals who pose a threat to public safety, health, or national security, repeat immigration law violators, and other individuals prioritized for removal. We also reduce the demand for illegal immigrants by conducting inspections, audits, and investigations of employers who hire illegal immigrants and administering tools such as E-Verify to facilitate employers' ability to hire eligible workers in compliance with immigration laws.

Arrest, detain, and remove criminals, fugitives, and other dangerous foreign nationals by leveraging federal information sharing and state, local, and federal criminal justice systems to take enforcement action based on priorities with regard to criminal aliens, and working

Credit: U.S. Customs and Border Protection

with the Department of Justice to ensure more timely hearing of immigration cases and appeals.

HIGHLIGHTED PERFORMANCE MEASURES

The table below presents a subset of the DHS performance measures associated with gauging results for Mission 3. For more information on these measures, along with a more extensive list of measures associated with this mission, please see the FY 2013–2015 Annual Performance Report at http://www.dhs.gov/xabout/budget/editorial_0430.shtm.

Mission 3: Enforce and Administer Our Immigration Laws				
Highlighted Performance Measures	Goal Alignment	Planned Targets		
		FY 2014	FY 2015	FY 2018
Average of processing cycle time (in months) for adjustment of status to permanent resident applications (I-485) (USCIS)	3.1	≤ 4.0	≤ 4.0	≤ 4.0
Average of processing cycle times (in months) for naturalization applications (N-400) (USCIS)	3.1	≤ 5.0	≤ 5.0	≤ 5.0
Overall customer service rating of the immigration process (USCIS)	3.1	85%	85%	85%
Number of convicted criminal aliens removed per fiscal year (ICE)	3.2	198,000	198,000	198,000
Average length of stay (in days) in detention of all convicted criminal aliens prior to removal from the United States (ICE)	3.2	≤ 34.5	≤ 34.5	≤ 32.5
Percent of detention facilities found in compliance with the national detention standards by receiving an acceptable inspection rating (ICE)	3.2	100%	100%	100%

MISSION 4: SAFEGUARD AND SECURE CYBERSPACE

Each and every day, the United States faces a myriad of threats in cyberspace, from the theft of trade secrets, payment card data, and other sensitive information through cyber intrusions to denial-of-service attacks against Internet websites and attempted intrusions of U.S. critical infrastructure. DHS works closely with government and private sector partners to strengthen cybersecurity capabilities, investigate cybercrime, and share actionable information to ensure a secure and resilient cyberspace that protects privacy and civil rights and civil liberties by design, supports innovation and economic growth, and supports public health and safety.

The 2014 Quadrennial Homeland Security Review outlines four strategic priorities to safeguard and secure cyberspace: 1) Strengthen the security and resilience of critical Infrastructure against cyber attacks and other hazards; 2) Secure the federal civilian government information technology enterprise; 3) Advance cyber law enforcement, incident response, and reporting capabilities; and 4) Strengthen the cyber ecosystem.

> ## MISSION PRIORITIES
>
> The following Mission Priorities represent the highest priority efforts for the Department of Homeland Security within Mission 4. While the Department will continue to work on all of the mission goals and objectives laid out in the 2014 Quadrennial Homeland Security Review and the 2014-2018 Strategic Plan, these are the top areas of focus in terms of investment, strategic and operational planning, and stakeholder engagement, and will be addressed through actions undertaken in one or more of the following DHS foundational activities: Joint Requirements Council, joint operational plans and operations, enhanced budget and investment processes, and focused strategic and analytic efforts.
>
> - **Reduce national cyber risk** through the Cybersecurity Framework, threat awareness, public awareness campaigns, and best practices, all of which increase the baseline capabilities of critical infrastructure.
>
> - **Enhance critical infrastructure security and resilience, with respect to physical and cyber risks,** by reducing vulnerabilities, sharing information on threat, consequences and mitigations, detecting malicious activity, promoting resilient critical infrastructure design, and partnering with critical infrastructure owners and operators.

GOAL 4.1: STRENGTHEN THE SECURITY AND RESILIENCE OF CRITICAL INFRASTRUCTURE AGAINST CYBER ATTACKS AND OTHER HAZARDS

The concept of critical infrastructure as discrete, physical assets has become outdated as everything becomes linked to cyberspace. This "cyber-physical convergence" has changed the risks to critical infrastructure in sectors ranging from energy and transportation to agriculture and healthcare. DHS coordinates with its private sector partners as well as with state, local, tribal, and territorial governments to share information and intelligence regarding cyber threats and vulnerabilities, foster development of trustworthy products and services, and encourage the adoption of best-in-class cybersecurity practices.

We will pursue the following strategies to strengthen the security and resilience of critical infrastructure against cyber attacks and other hazards:

Enhance the exchange of information and intelligence on risks to critical infrastructure and develop real-time situational awareness capabilities that ensure machine and human interpretation and visualization by increasing the volume, timeliness and quality of cyber threat reporting shared with the private sector and state, local, tribal, and territorial partners, and enabling the National Cybersecurity and Communications Integration Center (to receive information at "machine speed" by enabling networks to be more self-healing, using mathematics and analytics to mimic restorative processes that occur biologically.

Partner with critical infrastructure owners and operators to ensure the delivery of essential services and functions by building effective partnerships to set a national focus and determine collective actions, providing assistance to local and regional partners, and leveraging incentives to advance security and resilience, as described in the National Infrastructure Protection Plan: Partnering for Security and Resilience.

Identify and understand interdependencies and cascading impacts among critical systems by leveraging regional risk assessment programs, organization-specific assessment, asset- and network-specific assessment, and cross-sector risk assessments.

Collaborate with agencies and the private sector to identify and develop effective cybersecurity policies and best practices through voluntary collaboration with private sector owners and operators (including their partner associations, vendors, and others) and government entity counterparts.

Reduce vulnerabilities and promote resilient critical infrastructure design by identifying and promoting opportunities that build security and resilience into critical infrastructure as it is being developed and updated, rather than focusing solely on mitigating vulnerabilities present within existing critical infrastructure.

GOAL 4.2: SECURE THE FEDERAL CIVILIAN GOVERNMENT INFORMATION TECHNOLOGY ENTERPRISE

The Federal Government provides essential services and information on which many Americans rely. Not only must the government protect its own networks, it must serve as a role model to others in implementing security services. DHS itself plays a leading role in securing federal civilian networks, allowing the Federal Government to do its business securely. DHS partners with agencies to deploy products such as the EINSTEIN set of capabilities that provide perimeter network-based intrusion detection and prevention.

We will pursue the following strategies to secure the federal civilian government information technology enterprise:

Coordinate government purchasing of cyber technology to enhance cost-effectiveness by using strategically sourced tools and services such as the Continuous Diagnostics and Mitigation program.

Equip civilian government networks with innovative cybersecurity tools, information, and protections by supporting research and development and making the innovations from research and development available not only to the Federal Government but widely available across the public and private spheres.

Ensure government-wide policy and standards are consistently and effectively implemented and measured by promoting the adoption of enterprise-wide policy and best practices and working with interagency partners to develop government-wide requirements that can bring the full strength of the market to bear on existing and emergent vulnerabilities.

GOAL 4.3: ADVANCE CYBER LAW ENFORCEMENT, INCIDENT RESPONSE, AND REPORTING CAPABILITIES

Online criminal activity threatens the Internet's safe and secure use. Law enforcement performs an essential role in achieving our Nation's cybersecurity objectives by detecting, investigating, and preventing a wide range of cybercrimes, from theft and fraud to child exploitation, and apprehending and prosecuting those responsible. In addition to criminal prosecution, there is a need to rapidly detect and respond to incidents, including through the development of quarantine and mitigation strategies, as well as to quickly share incident information so that others may protect themselves. Safeguarding and securing cyberspace requires close coordination among federal law enforcement entities, network security experts, state, local, tribal, and territorial officials, and private sector stakeholders.

We will pursue the following strategies to advance cyber law enforcement, incident response, and reporting capabilities:

Respond to and assist in the recovery from cyber incidents by managing incident response activities through the National Cybersecurity and Communications Integration Center and fostering enhanced collaboration between law enforcement and network security officials to pre-plan responses to cyber incidents.

Deter, disrupt, and investigate cybercrime by 1) increasing the quantity and impact of cybercrime investigations; 2) partnering with other agencies to conduct high-profile criminal investigations, prioritize the recruitment and training of technical experts, and develop standardized methods; and 3) strengthening law enforcement agencies' ability to detect, investigate, and arrest those that make illicit use of cyberspace.

GOAL 4.4: STRENGTHEN THE CYBER ECOSYSTEM

Our entire society, from government and law enforcement to the private sector and members of the public, must work collaboratively to improve our network defense. Ensuring a healthy cyber ecosystem will require collaborative communities, innovative and agile security solutions, standardized and consistent processes to share information and best practices, sound policies and plans, meaningful protection of privacy, civil rights, and civil liberties, and development of a skilled workforce to ensure those policies and plans are implemented as intended.

We will pursue the following strategies to strengthen the cyber ecosystem:

Drive innovative and cost effective security products, services, and solutions throughout the cyber ecosystem by working with domestic and international partners across the public and private spheres, and across the science and policy communities to identify promising technology, policy and standards that enable robust, trust-based, automated sharing of cybersecurity information and collective action to limit the spread of incidents and minimize consequences.

Conduct and transition research and development, enabling trustworthy cyber infrastructure by supporting initiatives to develop promising new security technologies and techniques including: 1) security automation techniques to facilitate real-time incident response; 2) interoperability to support security cooperation across sectors; and 3) privacy enhancing authentication to enable better system protection.

Develop skilled cybersecurity professionals by promoting cybersecurity knowledge and innovation, developing Department-wide human capital strategies, policies, and programs intended to enhance the DHS cyber workforce, and working with public and private sector partners to increase the pipeline of highly qualified homeland security professionals through academic and federal training programs.

Enhance public awareness and promote cybersecurity best practices by promoting *National Cybersecurity Awareness Month* and the *Stop. Think. Connect.™ Campaign*, which raise awareness through collaborative outreach efforts and distributing materials, resources, and tips to promote cybersecurity.

Advance international engagement to promote capacity building, international standards, and cooperation by working to establish and deepen relationships with foreign computer incident response teams both bilaterally and through participation in operationally-focused multilateral fora, such as the Forum for Incident Response and Security Teams.

HIGHLIGHTED PERFORMANCE MEASURES

The table below presents a subset of the DHS performance measures associated with gauging results for Mission 4. For more information on these measures, along with a more extensive list of measures associated with this mission, please see the FY 2013–2015 Annual Performance Report at http://www.dhs.gov/xabout/budget/editorial_0430.shtm.

Mission 4: Safeguard and Secure Cyberspace				
Highlighted Performance Measures	Goal Alignment	Planned Targets		
		FY 2014	FY 2015	FY 2018
Percent of intelligence reports rated "satisfactory" or higher in customer feedback that enable customers to manage risks to cyberspace (AO)	4.1	94%	95%	95%
Percent of organizations that have implemented at least one cybersecurity enhancement after receiving a cybersecurity vulnerability assessment or survey (NPPD)	4.1	55%	60%	75%
Percent of traffic monitored for cyber intrusions at civilian Federal Executive Branch agencies (NPPD)	4.2	85.0%	87.0%	93.0%
Percent of incidents detected by the U.S. Computer Emergency Readiness Team for which targeted agencies are notified within 30 minutes (NPPD)	4.3	90.0%	92.0%	98.0%
Amount of dollar loss prevented by Secret Service cyber investigations (in millions) (USSS)	4.3	$900	$915	$975
Number of law enforcement individuals trained in cybercrime and cyber forensics both domestically and overseas (USSS)	4.3	1,000	1,000	1,000
Percent of planned cyber security products and services transitioned to government, commercial, and open sources (S&T)	4.4	65%	80%	80%

1

MISSION 5: STRENGTHEN NATIONAL PREPAREDNESS AND RESILIENCE

Despite ongoing vigilance and efforts to protect the United States and its citizens, major accidents, disruptions, and natural disasters, as well as deliberate attacks, will occur. The challenge is to build the capacity of American society to be resilient in the face of disruptions, disasters, and other crises. Our goals in this mission require us to: 1) enhance national preparedness; 2) mitigate hazards and vulnerabilities; 3) ensure effective emergency response; and 4) enable rapid recovery.

The 2014 Quadrennial Homeland Security Review reaffirms the Whole Community approach to national preparedness and resilience, which calls for the investment of everyone – not just the government – in preparedness efforts. Whole Community is a means by which emergency managers, organizational and community leaders, government officials, private and nonprofit sectors, faith-based and disability organizations, and the general public can collectively understand and assess the needs of their respective communities as well as determine the best ways to organize and strengthen their assets, capacities, and interests.

MISSION PRIORITIES

The following Mission Priorities represent the highest priority efforts for the Department of Homeland Security within Mission 5. While the Department will continue to work on all of the mission goals and objectives laid out in the 2014 Quadrennial Homeland Security Review and the 2014-2018 Strategic Plan, these are the top areas of focus in terms of investment, strategic and operational planning, and stakeholder engagement, and will be addressed through actions undertaken in one or more of the following DHS foundational activities: Joint Requirements Council, joint operational plans and operations, enhanced budget and investment processes, and focused strategic and analytic efforts.

- **Prepare the Nation for those threats and hazards that pose the greatest risk to the security of the Nation** by building and sustaining capabilities in order to achieve the National Preparedness Goal.

- **Ensure effective, unified incident response operations.**

GOAL 5.1: ENHANCE NATIONAL PREPAREDNESS

National preparedness underpins all efforts to safeguard and secure the Nation against those threats and hazards that pose the greatest risk. Presidential Policy Directive 8 calls for a National Preparedness Goal, which is "[a] secure and resilient Nation with the capabilities required across the Whole Community to prevent, protect against, mitigate, respond to, and recover from the threats and hazards that pose the greatest risk."

We will pursue the following strategies to enhance national preparedness:

Empower individuals and communities to strengthen and sustain their own preparedness by engaging public and community organizations through programs such as America's Preparathon! to build a collective understanding of their risks, the resources available to assist their preparations, and their roles and responsibilities in the event of a disaster.

Build and sustain core capabilities nationally to prevent, protect against, mitigate, respond to, and recover from all hazards by conducting such activities as: 1) fostering capability development by providing tools and technical assistance; 2) providing planning and reach-back expertise; 3) using grant programs such as the State Homeland Security Grant Program and the Urban Area Security Initiative (which collectively provide funds to state, local, tribal, territorial, and regional government and port, transit, and nonprofit entities); and 4) promoting the use of the National Planning Frameworks. These activities support the Department's intent to build and sustain a national integrated network of capabilities across all levels of government and to promote the involvement of the Whole Community in the

Nation's preparedness efforts.

Assist federal entities in the establishment of effective continuity programs that are regularly updated, exercised, and improved by administering the National Exercise Program, the cornerstone of a collective effort to test, improve, and assess national preparedness.

GOAL 5.2: MITIGATE HAZARDS AND VULNERABILITIES

DHS is uniquely positioned not only to support communities during a disaster, but also to enable partners to take steps that will decrease risk and mitigate future hazards before a disaster strikes. While risk cannot be totally eliminated, DHS can influence and support more positive outcomes in reducing risks. National risk management emphasizes focusing on those actions and interventions that reduce the greatest amount of strategic risk to the Nation.

We will pursue the following strategies to mitigate hazards and vulnerabilities:

Promote public and private sector awareness and understanding of community-specific risks by providing credible and actionable data and tools to support risk-informed decision making and incentivizing and facilitating investments to manage current and future risk.

Reduce vulnerability through standards, regulation, resilient design, effective mitigation, and disaster risk reduction measures by encouraging appropriate land use and adoption of building codes, while also applying engineering and planning practices in conjunction with advanced technology tools.

Prevent maritime incidents by establishing, and ensuring compliance with standards and regulations by licensing U.S. mariners, conducting and sharing findings of casualty investigations, and providing grants and support for government and nongovernment boating safety efforts.

GOAL 5.3: ENSURE EFFECTIVE EMERGENCY RESPONSE

DHS, primarily through the Federal Emergency Management Agency (FEMA) on land and the U.S. Coast Guard at sea, acts as the federal coordinator during disaster response, supporting state, local, tribal, territorial, and regional governments while working closely with nongovernmental organizations and the private sector to help leverage the resources they can bring to bear.

We will pursue the following strategies to ensure effective emergency response:

Provide timely and accurate information to individuals and communities to support public safety and inform appropriate actions by the public before, during, and after emergencies.

Conduct effective, unified incident response operations by following the National Response Framework, Second Edition; maximizing interagency coordination, information sharing, and preparation; and implementing initiatives to ensure a stable, flexible, and fully qualified disaster workforce.

Provide timely and appropriate disaster assistance through "survivor-centric" programs that support, streamline, and simplify the delivery of services for individuals and communities. DHS will strengthen capabilities and operationalize resource-sharing opportunities to achieve the greatest potential to change outcomes on the ground in catastrophic disasters.

Ensure effective emergency communications through the provision of technical communications capabilities enabling security, situational awareness, and operational decision making to manage emergencies under all circumstances.

GOAL 5.4: ENABLE RAPID RECOVERY

DHS plays a key role in facilitating recovery following a disaster by supplementing communities' recovery core capabilities; promoting infrastructure resilience guidelines and use of standards; and encouraging the development of continuity plans for communities, government entities, and private-sector organizations. The devastating effects of recent disasters have highlighted the need to reform our national approach to long-term recovery. Communities devastated by a disaster, particularly large-scale events such as Hurricane Sandy, face complex and difficult challenges including restoring economic viability, rebuilding infrastructure and public services, and establishing resilience against future hazards.

We will pursue the following strategies to enable rapid recovery:

Ensure continuity and restoration of essential services and functions by: 1) supplementing communities' recovery core capabilities; 2) encouraging the development of continuity plans for communities, government entities, and private-sector organizations; and 3) working to ensure continuity and rapid restoration of essential services.

Support and enable communities to rebuild stronger, smarter, and safer by following the National Disaster Recovery Framework and implementing programs that: 1) fund authorized federal disaster support activities; 2) support eligible reconstruction projects and disaster survivors; 3) provide subject matter experts to assist in planning and coordinating rebuilding efforts; and 4) focus on how best to restore, redevelop, and revitalize the health, social, economic, natural, and environmental fabric of the community and build a more resilient nation.

HIGHLIGHTED PERFORMANCE MEASURES

The table below presents a subset of the DHS performance measures associated with gauging results for Mission 5. For more information on these measures, along with a more extensive list of measures associated with this mission, please see the FY 2013–2015 Annual Performance Report at http://www.dhs.gov/xabout/budget/

Mission 5: Strengthen National Preparedness and Resilience				
			Planned Targets	
Highlighted Performance Measures	Goal Alignment	FY 2014	FY 2015	FY 2018
Percent of households that participated in a preparedness exercise or drill at their workplace, school, home, or other community location in the past year (FEMA)	5.1	42%	44%	50%
Percent of communities in high earthquake, flood, and wind-prone areas adopting disaster-resistant building codes (FEMA)	5.2	57%	61%	64%
Reduction in the potential cost of natural disasters to communities and their citizens (in billions) (FEMA)	5.2	$2.60	$2.60	$2.60
Percent of incident management and support actions necessary to stabilize an incident within 72 hours or by the agreed upon time (FEMA)	5.3	100%	100%	100%
Percent of orders for required life-sustaining commodities (meals, water, tarps, plastic sheeting, cots, blankets and generators) and key operational resources delivered by the agreed upon date (FEMA)	5.3	95%	95%	95%
Percent of people in imminent danger saved in the maritime environment (USCG)	5.3	100%	100%	100%
Percent of calls made by National Security/Emergency Preparedness users during emergency situations that DHS ensured were connected (NPPD)	5.3	100%	97%	98.5%
Percent of recovery services through Individual Assistance delivered to disaster survivors gauging the quality of program services, supporting infrastructure, and customer satisfaction following a disaster (FEMA)	5.4	92.0%	93.0%	96.0%
Percent of recovery services through Public Assistance delivered to communities gauging the quality of program services, supporting infrastructure, and customer satisfaction following a disaster (FEMA)	5.4	93.0%	93.0%	93.0%

Credit: U.S. Coast Guard

MATURE AND STRENGTHEN HOMELAND SECURITY

The Nation's experiences in the years since September 11, 2001 highlight the importance of joining efforts across all levels of society and government into a common homeland security. In considering the evolution of the Department and the ever-changing environment in which it operates, we have identified several key, cross-cutting functional areas of focus for action within the Department that must be accomplished in order for it to successfully execute its core missions. These functions, and the critical activities associated with them, serve as the supporting foundation that underpins all homeland security missions.

These goals also support the Unity of Effort Initiative, which builds important linkages between the Department's planning, programming, budgeting, and execution processes, ensuring that the Department invests and operates in a cohesive, unified fashion, and makes decisions that are transparent and collaborative to drive the Secretary's strategic guidance to results.

The following Mission Priorities represent the highest priority efforts for the Department of Homeland Security within Maturing and Strengthening Homeland Security. While the Department will continue to work on all of the mission goals and objectives laid out in the 2014 Quadrennial Homeland Security Review and the 2014-2018 Strategic Plan, these are the top areas of focus in terms of investment, strategic and operational planning, and stakeholder engagement, and will be addressed through actions undertaken in one or more of the following DHS foundational activities: Joint Requirements Council, joint operational plans and operations, enhanced budget and investment processes, and focused strategic and analytic efforts.

- **Enhance ability to analyze, fuse, and disseminate information and analysis** by improving integration of intelligence and operational activities — including screening and vetting practices and databases — investing in common enterprise solutions and services, and evolving toward real-time situational awareness, while protecting civil rights and civil liberties.

- **Enhance Unity of Effort** by strengthening forums for leadership decision-making, departmental management processes for investments, headquarters strategy, planning, and analytic capability, and coordinated operational planning.

- **Enhance employee morale** by recruiting, hiring, retain and developing a highly qualified, diverse, effective, mission-focused, and resilient workforce, and through providing expanded opportunities for professional growth and development.

GOAL 1: INTEGRATE INTELLIGENCE, INFORMATION SHARING, AND OPERATIONS

Rapidly evolving threats and hazards demand that DHS and our partners continually enhance situational awareness. As noted earlier, DHS is committed to integrating critical data sources while maintaining and safeguarding a culture that preserves privacy and civil rights and civil liberties.

We will pursue the following strategies to integrate intelligence, information sharing, and operations:

Enhance unity of regional operations coordination and planning by partnering with and supporting the national network of fusion centers in the form of deployed personnel, training, technical assistance, exercise support, security clearances, connectivity to federal systems, technology, and grant funding. DHS will also work to enhance intelligence enterprise support to Component and state, local, tribal, territorial and private sector homeland security missions by developing an integrated set of DHS intelligence enterprise priorities specific to collection and analysis and enhancing coordination among DHS headquarters, Component headquarters, and field elements.

Share homeland security information and analysis, threats, and risks by providing robust communications, coordination, information sharing, situational awareness capabilities, Department-level planning, and Department-level planning to homeland security partners.

Integrate counterintelligence, consistent with component and Departmental authorities, into all aspects of Department operations by utilizing the counterintelligence program management, counterintelligence analysis, and counterintelligence support and inquiries functions to safeguard homeland security-related national security information and other sensitive information.

Establish a common security mindset with domestic and international partners, through initiatives such as the DHS Common Operating Picture and the Homeland Security Information Network, which enable unity of effort with all homeland security partners, and through efforts to facilitate and integrate DHS's ability to share information with key foreign partners. Note that only trusted and vetted international partners receive access to properly screened sensitive information.

Preserve civil rights, civil liberties, privacy, oversight, and transparency in the execution of homeland security activities by creating appropriate policy as needed, advising Department leadership and personnel, assuring that the use of technologies sustain, and do not erode, privacy protections relating to the use, collection, and disclosure of personal information, and investigating and resolving any privacy, civil rights, or civil liberties complaints.

GOAL 2: ENHANCE PARTNERSHIPS AND OUTREACH

Homeland security is achieved through a shared effort among all partners, from corporations to nonprofits and American families. Recent events, including the 2010 Deepwater Horizon oil spill and Hurricane Sandy, highlight the fundamentally important relationship that DHS must foster and sustain with the private sector as well as state, local, tribal, territorial, and international partners. In addition, rapidly evolving or emerging operating domains such as cyberspace and the Arctic are demanding new approaches and models for how DHS partners to achieve homeland security objectives.

We will pursue the following strategies to enhance partnerships and outreach:

Promote regional response capacity and civil support by coordinating and advancing federal interaction with state, local, tribal, and territorial governments and by pursuing the Whole Community approach to build and sustain national preparedness.

Strengthen the ability of federal agencies to support homeland security missions by working with federal partners to ensure that Departmental roles, responsibilities, and interests are integrated with and incorporated into interagency activities.

Expand and extend governmental, nongovernmental, domestic, and international partnerships by building a Department-wide Community of Practice to synchronize the identification of potential partnership opportunities, develop a repository of partnerships and best practices, and serve as a consultative body to inform the exploration and formation of new public-private partnerships.

Further enhance the military-homeland security relationship by collaborating with the Department of Defense to pursue bilateral science and technology agreements; collaborate in information sharing and training; provide support for information systems Law Enforcement, and emergency and disaster response support; and develop international relationships.

GOAL 3: STRENGTHEN THE DHS INTERNATIONAL AFFAIRS ENTERPRISE IN SUPPORT OF HOMELAND SECURITY MISSIONS

DHS operates within a dynamic environment at home and abroad. The inherently transnational nature of homeland security missions necessitates a strong DHS international affairs enterprise that provides compatible visions of homeland security globally, a consistent and mutually beneficial cooperation with foreign partners, and an international footprint that maximizes mission effectiveness and return on investment.

We will pursue the following strategies to strengthen the DHS international affairs enterprise in support of homeland security missions:

Establish strategic priorities for the Department's international affairs enterprise by engaging across Components in areas including policy analysis, cross-regional coordination, and management of international affairs issues, to establish a single, accepted view of DHS international operations and engagements. Implementation plans will be developed to responsibly document how DHS Components will implement these strategic priorities in a unified manner.

Establish coordination and communication mechanisms across the DHS international affairs enterprise to ensure national, Departmental and Component priorities are synchronized and DHS's international engagements are fully utilized to achieve common objectives.

Technology and homeland security are inextricably linked. A vast array of interdependent information technology networks, systems, services, and resources enable communication, facilitate travel, power our homes, run our economy and provide essential government services. These systems provide enormous benefits to our society and economy, but they also create new risks and vulnerabilities. DHS must endeavor to keep pace with technology and leverage research and development toward homeland security goals.

We will pursue the following strategies to conduct homeland security research and development:

Employ scientific study to understand homeland security threats and vulnerabilities by pursuing a research and development strategy that is operationally focused, highly innovative, and founded on building partnerships among operators, scientists, and engineers, and by providing operational support, timely experiments, measurements, testing, evaluation, and analyses of homeland security significance.

Develop innovative approaches and effective solutions to mitigate threats and vulnerabilities by: 1) providing new capabilities through new technologies and operational process enhancements; 2) offering innovative systems-based solutions to complex problems; and 3) delivering the technical depth and reach to discover, adapt, and leverage scientific and engineering solutions developed by federal agencies and laboratories, state, local, and tribal governments, universities, and the private sector—across the United States and internationally.

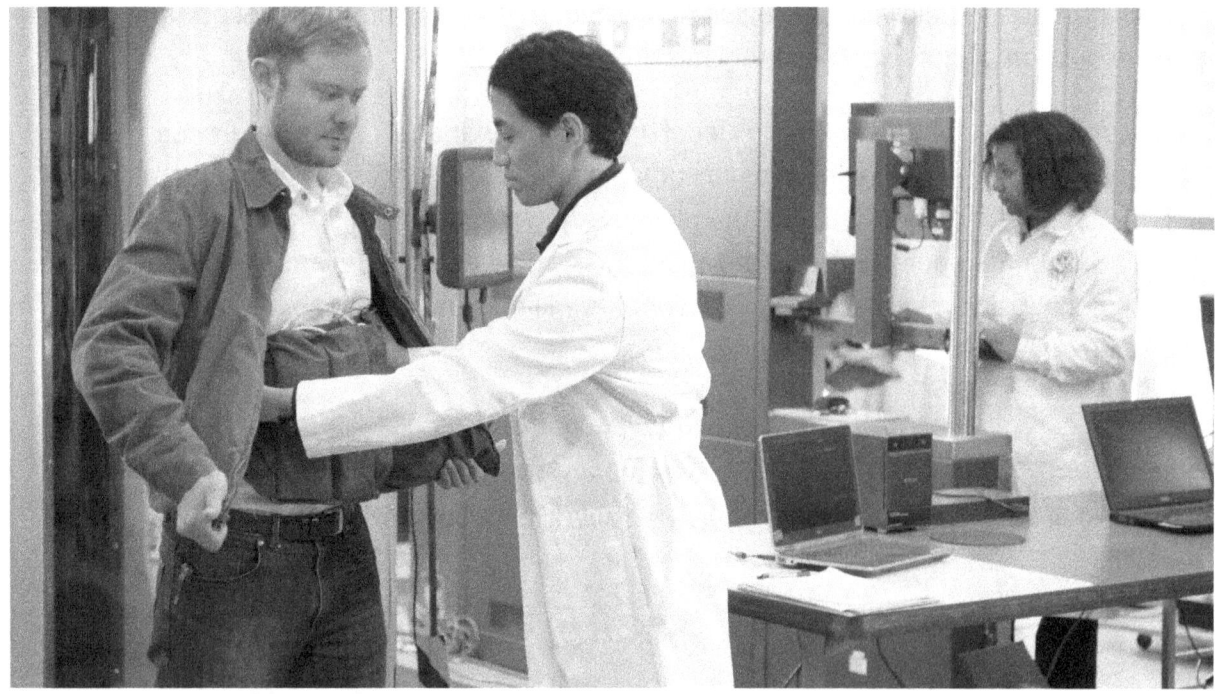

Leverage the depth of capacity in national labs, universities, and research centers by pursuing a mix of basic and applied research to deliver practical tools and analytic products that increase the effectiveness of components and save taxpayer dollars.

GOAL 5: ENSURE READINESS OF FRONTLINE OPERATORS AND FIRST RESPONDERS

In an era of decreasing budgets and resources, partners across the Department must strive to find and develop innovative solutions for training, exercising, and evaluating capabilities. Achieving baseline proficiency and maintaining high levels of readiness in homeland security-related individual and collective skills and knowledge are critical to a unified partnership of law enforcement, first responders, and other front-line operators.

We will pursue the following strategies to train and exercise frontline operators and first responders:

Support systems for training, exercising, and evaluating capabilities by pursuing integrated and cohesive cross-component training and evaluation.

Support law enforcement, first responder, and risk management training by providing coordinated, interoperable, and standardized law enforcement training to DHS and non-DHS federal agents/officers as well as to state, local, tribal and territorial and international entities.

GOAL 6: STRENGTHEN SERVICE DELIVERY AND MANAGE DHS RESOURCES

To support priority security requirements in a sustainable way, we must become more efficient and effective across a large and federated structure. As a Department, we must eliminate duplicative processes, develop common platforms, and purchase single solutions. In addition, the safety and security of our country can only be achieved through the hard work and dedication of our employees, with a diverse array of backgrounds, experiences, skills, and ideas. Our workforce serves as the foundation to ensure continued growth of our collective ability to prevent and respond to the threats facing the nation.

We will pursue the following strategies to strengthen service delivery and manage DHS resources:

Recruit, hire, retain, and develop a highly qualified, diverse, effective, mission-focused, and resilient workforce by implementing programs and resources that focus on four key objectives: 1) building an effective, mission-focused, diverse, and inspiring cadre of leaders; 2) recruiting a highly qualified and diverse workforce; 3) retaining an engaged workforce; and 4) solidifying a DHS culture of mission performance, adaptability, accountability, equity, and results.

Credit: Transportation Security Administration

Manage the integrated investment life cycle to ensure that strategic and analytically based decisions optimize mission performance by integrating performance with program plans and budgets that are well justified and balanced to support DHS priorities.

Manage and optimize financial resources, property/assets, procurements, security, and DHS IT by: 1) strengthening department service delivery in partnership with all components through integration teams to achieve affordable readiness; 2) pursuing strategic sourcing, small business utilization, and acquisition workforce management; and 3) maintaining a Department-wide IT infrastructure that is reliable, scalable, flexible, maintainable, accessible, secure, meets users' needs, and ensures operational excellence—from the workstation to the data center to the mission application.

Establish and execute a comprehensive and coordinated DHS health and medical system by providing medical guidance and Department-wide solutions to mitigate adverse health impacts and work-related health risks to support DHS employees and by embedding senior medical advisors with select operational components to develop and implement policies and procedures to improve force health protection, emergency medical services, global health security, and occupational health and wellness.

HIGHLIGHTED PERFORMANCE MEASURES

The table below presents a subset of the DHS performance measures associated with gauging results for the Mature and Strengthen area. For more information on these measures, along with a more extensive list of measures associated with this area, please see the FY 2013–2015 Annual Performance Report at http://www.dhs.gov/xabout/budget/editorial_0430.shtm.

Mature and Strengthen the Department				
Highlighted Performance Measures	Goal Alignment	Planned Targets		
		FY 2014	FY 2015	FY 2018
Percent of initial breaking homeland security blast calls initiated between the National Operations Center and designated homeland security partners within targeted timeframes (AO - OPS)	MS1	98%	98%	98%
Percent of Homeland Security Advanced Research Projects Agency (HSARPA) program milestones that are met, as established in the fiscal year's budget execution plan (S&T)	MS4	75%	75%	75%
Percent of Partner Organizations that agree the FLETC training programs address the right skills (e.g., critical knowledge, key skills and techniques, attitudes/behaviors) needed for their officers/agents to perform their law enforcement duties (FLETC)	MS5	97%	97%	97%
Percent of veteran hires among total DHS hires in each fiscal year (DMO - CHCO)	MS6	25%	25%	25%
Percent of environmentally preferable and sustainable purchasing actions (DMO - CPO)	MS6	95%	95%	95%
Percent of Equal Employment Opportunity complaints timely adjudicated (DMO - CRCL)	MS6	40%	45%	60%
Percent reduction in scope 1 & 2 greenhouse gas emissions (DMO - CRSO)	MS6	5%	7%	19%

APPENDIX A: MISSION PROGRAMS BY GOAL

The table below identifies the DHS programs that contribute to each goal. A mission program is defined as an organized set of activities acting together to accomplish high-level outcomes. Mission programs are the operational processes, skills, technology, human capital, and other resources leveraged to achieve Department missions, goal, and sub-goals. Mission programs are those programs that reside in the Future Years Homeland Security (FYHSP) system.

Mission 1
Goal 1.1
AO
- Analysis and Operations

CBP
- Integrated Operations
- Intelligence and Targeting
- Management and Administration
- Securing America's Borders
- Securing and Expediting Trade
- Securing and Expediting Travel

FLETC
- Law Enforcement Training

ICE
- Automation Modernization
- Homeland Security Investigations (HSI)

ST
- Research, Development, and Innovation

TSA
- In Flight Security
- Intermodal Assessments and Enforcement
- Intermodal Screening Operations
- Management and Administration

USCG
- Cross-Cutting Capital Investments and Maintenance
- Defense Operations
- Maritime Prevention
- Maritime Security Operations
- Mission Support

Goal 1.2
AO
- Analysis and Operations

CBP
- Integrated Operations
- Intelligence and Targeting
- Management and Administration

DNDO
- Domestic Rad/Nuc Detection, Forensics and Prevention Capability

NPPD
- Infrastructure Protection

OHA
- Health Threats Resilience

ST
- Research, Development, and Innovation

TSA
- Intermodal Assessments and Enforcement

USCG
- Cross-Cutting Capital Investments and Maintenance
- Maritime Security Operations
- Mission Support

Goal 1.3

AO

- Analysis and Operations

CBP

- Integrated Operations
- Intelligence and Targeting
- Management and Administration
- Securing America's Borders

FLETC

- Law Enforcement Training

NPPD

- Federal Protective Service
- Infrastructure Protection

USCG

- Cross-Cutting Capital Investments and Maintenance
- Defense Operations
- Maritime Prevention
- Maritime Security Operations
- Mission Support

USSS

- Criminal Investigations
- Information Integration and Technology Transformation
- Management and Administration
- Protection
- Protective Intelligence
- Rowley Training Center

Mission 2

Goal 2.1

AO

- Analysis and Operations

CBP

- Integrated Operations
- Intelligence and Targeting
- Management and Administration
- Securing America's Borders
- Securing and Expediting Trade

- Securing and Expediting Travel

FLETC

- Law Enforcement Training

NPPD

- Office of Biometric Identity Management

ST

- Research, Development, and Innovation

USCG

- Cross-Cutting Capital Investments and Maintenance
- Defense Operations
- Maritime Law Enforcement
- Mission Support

Goal 2.2

CBP

- Integrated Operations
- Intelligence and Targeting
- Management and Administration
- Securing and Expediting Trade
- Securing and Expediting Travel

FLETC

- Law Enforcement Training

ICE

- Homeland Security Investigations (HSI)
- Management and Administration

ST

- Research, Development, and Innovation

TSA

- Intermodal Assessments and Enforcement

USCG

- Cross-Cutting Capital Investments and Maintenance

APPENDIX A

- Marine Transportation System Management
- Maritime Law Enforcement
- Maritime Prevention
- Mission Support

Goal 2.3
CBP
- Intelligence and Targeting
- Securing America's Borders
FLETC
- Law Enforcement Training
ICE
- Automation Modernization
- Homeland Security Investigations (HSI)
ST
- Research, Development, and Innovation
USCG
- Cross-Cutting Capital Investments and Maintenance
- Defense Operations
- Maritime Law Enforcement
- Mission Support

Mission 3
Goal 3.1
ICE
- Homeland Security Investigations (HSI)
NPPD
- Office of Biometric Identity Management
USCIS
- Adjudication Services
- Citizenship
- Crosscutting Investments
- Immigration Status Verification
- Information and Customer Service
- Management and Administration

Goal 3.2
CBP
- Integrated Operations
- Intelligence and Targeting
- Management and Administration
- Securing America's Borders
FLETC
- Law Enforcement Training
ICE
- Automation Modernization
- Construction
- Enforcement and Removal Operations (ERO)
- Homeland Security Investigations (HSI)
- Management and Administration
NPPD
- Office of Biometric Identity Management
ST
- Research, Development, and Innovation
USCG
- Cross-Cutting Capital Investments and Maintenance
- Maritime Law Enforcement
- Mission Support
USCIS
- Crosscutting Investments
- Immigration Security and Integrity
- Immigration Status Verification
- Management and Administration

Mission 4
Goal 4.1
AO
- Analysis and Operations
FLETC
- Law Enforcement Training
ICE
- Homeland Security Investigations (HSI)

NPPD
- Cybersecurity and Communications
- Federal Protective Service
- Infrastructure Protection
- Office of Cyber and Infrastructure Analysis

Goal 4.2
NPPD
- Cybersecurity and Communications

Goal 4.3
FLETC
- Law Enforcement Training
NPPD
- Cybersecurity and Communications
ST
- Research, Development, and Innovation
USSS
- Criminal Investigations
- Information Integration and Technology Transformation
- Management and Administration
- Rowley Training Center

Goal 4.4
FLETC
- Law Enforcement Training
NPPD
- Cybersecurity and Communications
ST
- Research, Development, and Innovation

Mission 5
Goal 5.1
AO
- Analysis and Operations

CBP
- Integrated Operations
FEMA
- Management and Administration
- Mission Program Support
- Preparedness
- Protection
- Recovery
- Response
FLETC
- Law Enforcement Training
OHA
- Health Threats Resilience
- Workforce Health and Medical Support
ST
- Research, Development, and Innovation
USCG
- Cross-Cutting Capital Investments and Maintenance
- Maritime Response
- Mission Support

Goal 5.2
FEMA
- Management and Administration
- Mission Program Support
- Mitigation
FLETC
- Law Enforcement Training
ICE
- Homeland Security Investigations (HSI)
- Management and Administration
ST
- Acquisition and Operations Support
USCG
- Cross-Cutting Capital Investments and

APPENDIX A

Maintenance
- Marine Transportation System Management
- Maritime Prevention
- Mission Support

Goal 5.3
AO
- Analysis and Operations

CBP
- Integrated Operations
- Securing America's Borders

FEMA
- Management and Administration
- Mission Program Support
- Preparedness
- Protection
- Recovery
- Response

FLETC
- Law Enforcement Training

ICE
- Homeland Security Investigations (HSI)
- Management and Administration

NPPD
- Cybersecurity and Communications

OHA
- Workforce Health and Medical Support

ST
- Research, Development, and Innovation

USCG
- Cross-Cutting Capital Investments and Maintenance
- Maritime Response
- Mission Support

Goal 5.4
AO
- Analysis and Operations

CBP
- Integrated Operations

FEMA
- Management and Administration
- Mission Program Support
- Mitigation
- Protection
- Recovery
- Response

FLETC
- Law Enforcement Training

ST
- Management and Administration
- Research, Development, and Innovation

USCG
- Cross-Cutting Capital Investments and Maintenance
- Maritime Response
- Mission Support

Maturing and Strengthening
Goal 1
AO
- Analysis and Operations

CBP
- Management and Administration

DMO
- Mission Support - Office of the Secretary and Executive Management
- Mission Support - Under Secretary for Management

FEMA
- Management and Administration

ICE
- Homeland Security Investigations (HSI)
- Management and Administration

OHA
- Health Threats Resilience

ST
- Research, Development, and Innovation

USCG
- Mission Support

Goal 2
AO
- Analysis and Operations

DMO
- Mission Support - Office of the Secretary and Executive Management

OHA
- Health Threats Resilience

ST
- Acquisition and Operations Support

USCG
- Mission Support

USSS
- Criminal Investigations

Goal 3
DMO
- Mission Support - Office of the Secretary and Executive Management

ST
- Acquisition and Operations Support

USCG
- Mission Support

Goal 4
ST
- Laboratory Facilities
- University Programs

USCG
- Mission Support

Goal 5
DMO
- Mission Support - Office of the Secretary and Executive Management

FLETC
- Accreditation
- Law Enforcement Training

OHA
- Workforce Health and Medical Support

ST
- Acquisition and Operations Support

Goal 6
AO
- Analysis and Operations

CBP
- Integrated Operations
- Management and Administration

DMO
- Mission Support - Office of the Secretary and Executive Management
- Management and Administration - Office of the Secretary and Executive Management
- Management and Administration - Under Secretary for Management

DNDO
- Management and Administration

FEMA
- Management and Administration

FLETC
- Management and Administration

ICE
- Management and Administration

IG
- Audits, Inspections, and Investigations
- Management and Administration

APPENDIX A

NPPD
- Management and Administration

OHA
- Management and Administration
- Workforce Health and Medical Support

ST
- Management and Administration
- University Programs

TSA
- Management and Administration

USCG
- Management and Administration
- Mission Support

USCIS
- Adjudication Services
- Management and Administration

USSS
- Management and Administration

AO	Analysis and Operations
CBP	U.S. Customs and Border Protection
DMO	Department Management and Operations
DNDO	Domestic Nuclear Detection Office
FEMA	Federal Emergency Management Agency
FLETC	Federal Law Enforcement Training Centers
ICE	Immigration and Customs Enforcement
IG	Inspector General
NPPD	National Protection and Programs Directorate
OHA	Office of Health Affairs
ST	Science and Technology
TSA	Transportation Security Administration
USCIS	United States Citizenship and Immigration Services
USCG	United States Coast Guard
USSS	United States Secret Service

APPENDIX B

The strategic decisions of the Department's senior leadership are only as good as the processes that support and give effect to those decisions through investments and in the conduct of operations. Historically, DHS has generally developed and executed Component-centric requirements, which has resulted in inefficient use of limited resources. Much work has been done to date in the areas of joint requirements analysis, program and budget review, and acquisition oversight, including an effort over the past four years by the DHS Management Directorate to improve the Department's overall acquisitions process, reforming even the earliest phase of the investment life cycle where requirements are first conceived and developed. To make further progress, the Department will make use of existing structures and create new capability, where needed, as revealed by the recent Integrated Investment Life Cycle Management pilot study. That effort tested process linkages and underscored the need to further strengthen all elements of the process, particularly the up-front development of strategy, planning, and joint requirements so that these elements are developed based on DHS-wide missions and functions, rather than focusing on those of an individual Component.

The Department is capitalizing on these previous efforts and broadening them in the Unity of Effort Initiative. This effort focuses on improving the DHS planning, programming, budgeting, and execution processes through strengthened Departmental structures and increased capability. In making these changes, the Department will have better traceability between strategic objectives, budgeting, acquisition decisions, operational plans, and mission execution to improve Departmental cohesiveness and operational effectiveness—realizing the vision of a true "guidance to results" framework for DHS. Individual components have taken this commitment to heart, as evidenced, for example, by the U.S. Coast Guard Unity of Effort Management Imperative.

Specifically, the Department is prioritizing its efforts on the following focus areas that are intended to build organizational capacity to develop action plans and implement change:

Departmental Leadership Forums: The Secretary (Senior Leaders Council) and Deputy Secretary (Deputy's Management Action Group) chair twice-monthly forums of the DHS Components and select headquarters counterparts, gathering in an environment of trust, and openly placing on the table issues, arguments, and disagreements concerning the Department's most challenging issues. These meetings, convened to discuss issues of overall policy, strategy, operations and Departmental guidance, are already moving forward specific initiatives in joint requirements development, program and budget review, acquisition reform, operational planning, and joint operations.

Departmental Management Processes for Investments: The DHS Chief Financial Officer is strengthening and enhancing the Department's programming and budgeting process by incorporating the results of strategic analysis and joint requirements planning into portfolios for review by cross-component issue teams. Substantive, large-scale alternative choices have been presented to the Deputies Management Action Group as part of the annual budget development. This review process also includes the Department's existing programmatic and budgetary structure, not just new investments, as well as the ability for DHS to project the impact of current decisions on resource issues such as staffing, capital acquisitions, operations and maintenance, and similar issues that impact the Department's future ability to fulfill its mission responsibilities.

In addition, the Department has established a joint requirements council to lead an enhanced DHS joint requirements process. This new council has already begun to identify priority gaps and overlaps in Departmental capability needs, and will use DHS's analytic capabilities to develop feasible technical alternatives to meet capability needs, and provide them, along with recommendations for creation of joint programs and joint acquisitions to meet Departmental mission needs, where appropriate, for senior leader decision.

Finally, Under Secretary of Management has conducted a full review of the Department's acquisition oversight framework and is taking action to update the processes, ultimately resulting in a transparent, comprehensive continuum of activities that link and integrate Departmental strategy and planning, development of joint requirements, programming and budgeting decisions, capital investment planning, and the effective and efficient execution of major acquisitions and programs.

DHS Headquarters Strategy, Planning, and Analytical Capability: The Department has taken action to focus its Departmental level strategy, planning, and analytical capability to more robustly understand and coordinate with DHS Component level functions to support more effective DHS-wide operations. This enhanced capability better supports Secretary in executing the responsibility to understand from a Departmental perspective how the activities, operations, and programs of each individual Component fit together in order to best meet Departmental mission responsibilities in a constrained resource environment. The goal in focusing the collective DHS Headquarters capability, which will harness a number of existing analytic cells throughout DHS, is not to eliminate the need for Component-level planning or analysis. To the contrary, this new, focused DHS Headquarters capability will work together with the planning and analytical organizations within each Component to develop a comprehensive picture of the Department's mission responsibilities and functional capabilities, and to identify points of friction or gaps, thus framing the corresponding choices that must be made. This capability will be integrated into, not created and employed in isolation from, existing Departmental functions that are critical to day-to-day mission execution and mission support activities.

Departmental Processes for Enhancing Coordinated Operations: The strategic decisions of the Department's senior leadership and the investments our Department makes in current and future capabilities will only be effective if cross-department operations are planned and executed in a coordinated fashion. Many DHS operations are conducted solely by a single Component, although successful examples of joint operational activities exist in seaports such as Charleston, SC, Miami, FL, San Diego, CA, and Seattle, WA, and through organizations chartered under the National Interdiction Command and Control Plan such as Joint Interagency Task Force-South in Key West, FL, the El Paso Intelligence Center in El Paso, TX, and the Air and Marine Operations Center in Riverside, CA.

Supporting this objective, the Department is exploring, concurrent with the development of joint operational plans, additional strategic alternatives for future coordinated operations. Enhancing the effectiveness and unity of DHS operations to better fulfill the Department's mission responsibilities is the primary reason for making these important changes, which represent a degree of departure from current DHS and Component level approaches to management and operations. But in adding structure and transparency, combined with collaborative, forthright senior leader engagement the Department will build together a stronger, more unified, and enduring DHS.

END EFFECT – WHAT SUCCESS LOOKS LIKE

Unity of Effort is the state of integrating DHS organizations: *the whole is so much more powerful than the sum of the parts.* This will be achieved through integrated governance, strategy, processes, analysis, and culture.

INTEGRATED GOVERNANCE
Managing and implementing key enterprise decisions. Key success factors:
- **Leadership accountability**; roles and responsibilities are clear, understood, and effective
- **Delegations of authorities** are clear, understood and effective
- **Priorities** support DHS enterprise
- **Data driven, transparent, objective** decision making
- Executive decisions are **communicated and implemented**
- **Coordinated, collaborative management and execution**

INTEGRATED STRATEGY

Defining and implementing DHS strategic intent. Key success factors:

- Strategic development process is **documented, transparent, timely, synchronized, repeatable, and balanced**
- **Authorities, roles, and responsibilities** are clearly articulated and documented
- **Strategy drives resource planning (PPB&E) and joint operational planning**, and aligns with timelines
- **Planning emphasizes** long-term (e.g., QHSR) and mid-term (e.g., FYHSP) **strategic intent**
- **Implementation** aligns with strategic intent
- Feedback loop rapidly **incorporates lessons learned** (e.g., capability gaps) back into planning cycle

INTEGRATED PROCESSES

Synchronizing DHS processes to provide collaborative and efficient delivery of services. Key success factors:

- Processes are **documented, transparent, timely, synchronized, stable, and repeatable**
- Process methodology is **agile and responsive**
- Processes include **quantitative measures**
- **Incorporates strategy**, capabilities and requirements, PPB&E, and acquisitions
- Feedback loop rapidly **incorporates lessons learned** back into process

INTEGRATED ANALYSIS

Integrating accurate and relevant information to inform DHS decision makers. Key success factors:

- Analysis is **documented, transparent, synchronized, and repeatable**
- Analysis is **timely for decision making**
- Measures are **quantifiable, repeatable, and actionable**
- Strategic analysis and lessons learned **inform operational planning**
- Operational analysis **emphasizes capabilities** and informs **joint requirement development**

INTEGRATED CULTURE

Supporting DHS common goals. Key success factors:

- Component priorities **support overarching DHS missions**
- **Responsive** to homeland security enterprise demands
- **Commitment to collaborate** and coordinate capabilities, assets and other resources

APPENDIX C

APPENDIX C: AGENCY PRIORITY GOALS

During FY 2014–2015, the Department will continue to pursue the priorities expressed in the FY 2012–2014 Agency Priority Goals but is maturing the goals to drive results in areas identified as Administration priorities. The following tables summarize the FY 2014–2015 Agency Priority Goals. Results for these goals will be available quarterly on www.performance.gov.

Agency Priority Goal 1: Strengthen Aviation Security Counterterrorism Capabilities and Improve the Passenger Experience by Using Intelligence Driven Information and Risk-Based Decisions	
Goal Statement	By September 30, 2015, TSA will expand the use of risk-informed security initiatives to increase the percentage of travelers eligible for expedited screening at airports to 50 percent and enhance the passenger experience.
Overview	TSA performs and oversees security operations at the Nation's airports, screening more than 650 million passengers annually, to ensure the freedom of movement of people and commerce. In an effort to strengthen aviation security while enhancing the passenger experience, TSA is focusing on risk-informed, intelligence-driven security procedures and enhancing its use of technology. Since 2011, the Agency has implemented several risk-informed initiatives including implementation of the TSA Pre✓™ expedited screening program; the nationwide implementation of modified screening protocols for passengers 12 and younger, passengers 75 and over, and active-duty service members; expediting physical screening of Veterans on chartered Honor Flights; and providing modified screening to Wounded Warriors. A number of initiatives will further enable TSA to reach its goal of expanding expedited screening for known populations in order to focus on those that are unknown including development and deployment of the TSA Pre✓™ Application and TSA Risk Assessment programs; expansion of TSA Pre✓™ participation to international air carriers; continued expansion of the Known Crewmember program; and developing operational policies, procedures, and other activities such as the evolution of checkpoint screening technologies to support deployment of Risk Assessments that will grow the volume of passengers eligible for expedited screening. As of December 2013, on a weekly basis, more than 32% of passengers receive some form of expedited screening, and TSA expects to continue to increase that number. While driving the growth of eligible populations is key to the initiative's long-term success, TSA faces challenges in aligning, planning, and executing activities for incorporating these various populations. The success of achieving TSA's risk-informed security milestones is in many ways reliant upon external and internal partners that TSA continues to work with to mitigate these challenges.

Agency Priority Goal 2: Enforce and Administer Our Immigration Laws Through Prioritized Detention	
Goal Statement	By September 30, 2015, ICE will increase criminal alien removals, as a percentage of total removals, by 5 percent.
Overview	U.S. Immigration and Customs Enforcement (ICE) is committed to identifying, arresting, detaining, prosecuting, and removing aliens who present a danger to national security or are a risk to public safety, as well as those who otherwise undermine the integrity of our immigration laws and border control efforts. These include, but are not limited to aliens engaged in or suspected of terrorism or espionage; violent criminals, felons, and repeat offenders; and organized criminal gang members. Also critical to ICE enforcement priorities are recent illegal border crossers. This goal is a continuation of the effort that began in FY 2012 to increase efficiencies in the process of detaining and removing illegal aliens. The next two years will be to showcase ICE's abilities to remove criminal aliens from the United States. These efforts include identifying and apprehending at-large criminal aliens and expanding coverage in jails and prisons in order to identify and process removable incarcerated foreign-born detainees. Through the use of Secure Communities, ICE continues to work with the Federal Bureau of Investigation (FBI) to identify criminal aliens who have been booked into custody, without imposing new of additional requirements on state and local law enforcement. This is accomplished by checking fingerprints submitted to the FBI by the arresting law enforcement agency against the DHS's immigration database to determine if the suspect has a criminal or immigration history, and/or is otherwise removable from the United States due to a criminal conviction. ICE has expanded the exercise of prosecutorial discretion through initiatives such as the case-by-case review, which improves efficiencies by identifying and eliminating low-priority cases clogging the immigration system. The use of prosecutorial discretion also allows ICE to prioritize the use of its enforcement personnel, detention space, and removal assets to ensure that the aliens it removes represent, as much as reasonably possible, ICE enforcement priorities, namely the promotion of national security, border security, public safety and the integrity of the immigration system.

Agency Priority Goal 3: Ensure Resilience to Disasters by Strengthening Disaster Preparedness and Response Capabilities	
Goal Statement	By September 30, 2015, 39 states and territories will demonstrate improvement in achieving their core capability targets established through their Threat and Hazard Identification and Risk Assessment (THIRA).
Overview	To enhance national preparedness and resilience, FEMA established THIRA to provide a common approach for identifying and assessing risks and documenting their associated impacts. Developing an understanding of risks from natural, technological, and human-caused threats and hazards allows a community to make informed decisions about how to manage risk and develop needed capabilities. In addition, states and territories assess their current capability and set targets for improvement for preventing, protecting against, mitigating, responding to, and recovering from these threats and hazards. FEMA expects states and territories to mature and demonstrate improvement in achieving their capability targets over the next 2 years through their THIRAs.

www.ingramcontent.com/pod-product-compliance
Lightning Source LLC
Chambersburg PA
CBHW081115280526
45787CB00007B/2837